SCHOLASTIC

NO BORING PRACTICE, PLEASE!

VOCABULARY

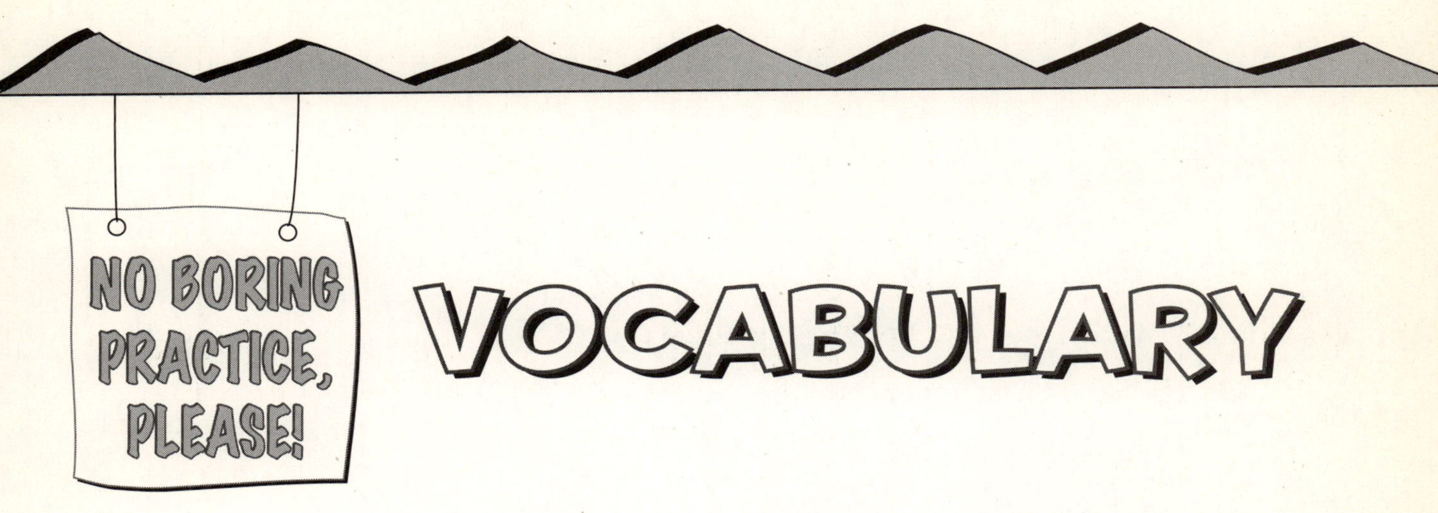

Reproducible Practice Pages PLUS Easy-to-Score Quizzes
That Boost Kids' Word Power and Comprehension

by Harold Jarnicki

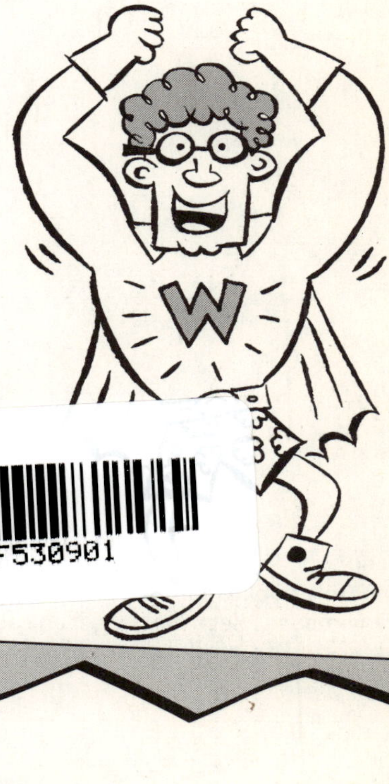

New York • Toronto • London • Auckland • Sydney
New Delhi • Mexico City • Hong Kong • Buenos Aires

Teaching Resources

Cover by Jaime Lucero
Cover illustrations Mike Moran
Interior design by NEO Grafika
Illustrations by Kelly Kennedy

ISBN 0-439-53148-9

Printed in the U.S.A.

1 2 3 4 5 6 7 8 9 10 40 12 11 10 09 08 07 06 05

Introduction 4
What Is Vocabulary? 6
Thesaurus Power 7
Thesaurus Hunt 8
Presto! The Prefix 9
Negative Prefixes 10
Positively Negative 11
Extraordinary Prefixes 12
Ultra-Cool X-Word 13
Let's Get Retro! Prefix Review 14
Quickie Quiz: Prefixes 16
Suffix Rocks! 17
Suffix Math 18
X-Word-Ology 20
Be a Suffix Sleuth 21
Let's Get Retro! Suffix Review 22
Quickie Quiz: Suffixes 24
Eponyms: It's All in the Name! 25
WOW! Palindromes! 27
What an Oxymoron! 28
Let's Get Retro! Eponym and Palindrome Review 29
Quickie Quiz: Eponyms, Palindromes, Oxymoron 30
Sound Out Homophones 31
Home in on Homographs 33
Commonly Confused Words 34
Put It in Context 35
Quickie Quiz: Homophones, Homographs, and More 36
The Synonym/Antonym Analogy Adventure 38
The Relationship Analogy Adventure 39
The "Part of" Analogy Adventure . . . 41
Quickie Quiz: Analogies 43
Answer Key 45

Introduction

Imagine a classroom where students do not slump in their seats every time you announce it's time for vocabulary; where vocabulary lessons and practice bring exciting opportunities along with a couple of laughs and a little competition; where students get emotionally involved in the fundamentals of vocabulary, and improvement is proudly displayed by students and recognized by teachers and parents.

You might think such a classroom is merely a figment of my imagination or a fantasy of some ambitiously naive first-year education grad. I can boldly claim that such is not the case. I have been teaching for about 20 years and, with the help of some games, a few jokes, and other gimmicks, have witnessed students get excited about vocabulary, spelling, grammar, and more.

The No Boring Practice, Please! series is an extension of my classroom and one humble step toward helping kids do what comes naturally — learn. If you're ready to add spice to your vocabulary lessons, then this book is for you.

Carefully structured as a good basic course of study, the recipe for each lesson is simple. *No Boring Practice, Please! Vocabulary* dishes up straight vocabulary practice with a dash (or splash) of fun. Inside you'll find a concoction of reproducible pages that cover prefixes, suffixes, synonyms, antonyms, analogies, homophones, and more. Flavored with engaging illustrations and an edgy design, each practice page is easy for kids to swallow. Best of all, you can serve these pages with only a minimal amount of teacher instruction.

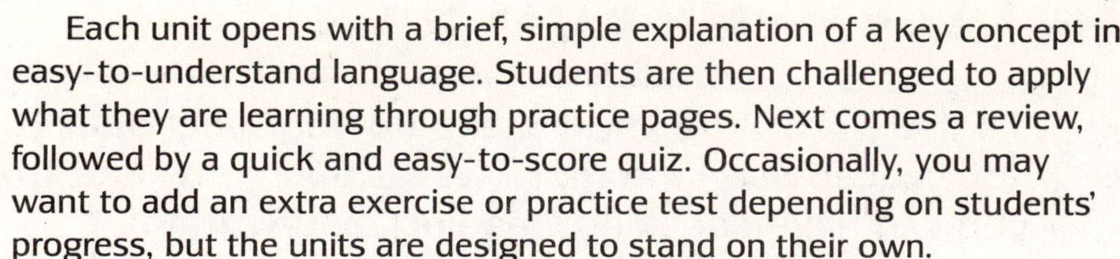

Each unit opens with a brief, simple explanation of a key concept in easy-to-understand language. Students are then challenged to apply what they are learning through practice pages. Next comes a review, followed by a quick and easy-to-score quiz. Occasionally, you may want to add an extra exercise or practice test depending on students' progress, but the units are designed to stand on their own.

You may wonder what inspired me to write this book—and the rest of the No Boring Practice, Please! series. Let me start at the beginning. As a baby boomer's hyperactive kid, I wasn't a huge fan of school. Sitting at a desk most of the day was tough enough. Add a generous helping of dry vocabulary practice and my eyes would glaze over, roll back in my head, and send me into a near comatose state where hands on clocks ceased to move.

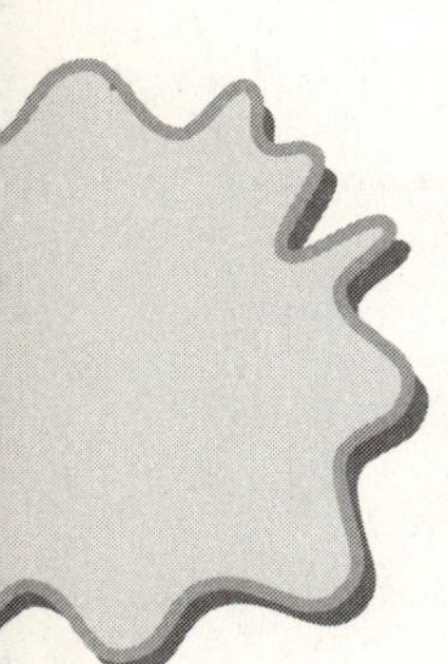

Years passed. After a less-than-stellar career in rock 'n' roll, I decided the teaching profession was a more lucrative gig. I had two specific goals: (1) to become the teacher I never had; and (2) to add a little rock 'n' roll to the school system.

Like it or not, we are teaching a new breed of children—one that watches more than four hours of values-distorting TV each day, plays mindless video games on a regular basis, and gobbles up entertainment far more than nutriment. We welcome these media-savvy kids into our classrooms and expect them to get excited about root words, homophones, and analogies. Let's get real!

This is what drives the No Boring Practice, Please! series. The series is academically sound and rich in language-skill development, but all this learning is disguised by a hip design and comical illustrations that have lots of kid appeal. Think of the series as whole-grain oats packaged in a box of tutti-frutti breakfast cereal.

I know that students can get excited about doing well in vocabulary, and I feel gratified to be part of the process. I hope the No Boring Practice, Please! series helps teach and inspire.

May the force be with you.

Sincerely,
Harold Jarnicki

Name ____________________________________

What Is Vocabulary?

All the words you know make up your **vocabulary**. The bigger your vocabulary, the more words you know and the more fun you can have speaking, reading, and writing!

Check out this ***bodacious*** activity. Wow your friends with your ***titanic*** vocabulary! They'll think your brain is absolutely ***colossal***. We guarantee they will be ***astonished*** by your ***extreme*** intelligence.

bodacious – remarkable

astonish – to amaze

titanic – having extraordinary power or size

colossal – massively large

extreme – great

Try it! **List four of your favorite words and write each word's meaning. Then use the word in a sentence that helps express the word's meaning.**

Favorite Word 1: ____________________ **Meaning:** ____________________

Sentence: ____

Favorite Word 2: ____________________ **Meaning:** ____________________

Sentence: ____

Favorite Word 3: ____________________ **Meaning:** ____________________

Sentence: ____

Favorite Word 4: ____________________ **Meaning:** ____________________

Sentence: ____

Name ______________________________

Thesaurus Power

Thesaurus? Is that some kind of extinct reptile?

A **thesaurus** is a book of synonyms and antonyms. Synonyms are words that mean the same thing. Antonyms are words with opposite meanings.

Synonym sample: *colossal*, *massive*, *huge*
Antonym sample: *hot* and *cold*

A ***thesaurus*** can help make your writing more interesting, attention-grabbing, and powerful. With a thesaurus you can take an ordinary word and *PRESTO! CHANGE-O!* make it more exciting.

Take this simple sentence: **Guido ran down the street after his dog.**
Open a thesaurus and the sentence can change to:

- Guido **darted** down the street after his dog.
- Guido **dashed** down the street after his dog.
- Guido **zoomed** down the street after his dog.

Replace the underlined word with a powerful, attention-grabbing word from the thesaurus. Make sure the word fits the sentence.

Example: "Let's go!" ~~shouted~~ **bellowed** Coach Beefy.

1. It is a nice day.
2. We had a delicious meal.
3. That is a big building.
4. Mrs. Jovial is always so happy.
5. The stage lights are bright.
6. Bozo was angry when he fell in the mud.
7. Eating breakfast makes me feel strong.
8. Wow, that was a nice try!
9. What is your plan, Secret Agent Map?
10. Professor Obtuse is very smart.

Ha! Ha! FUNNY Word Search
Find six synonyms for the word *funny* and list them below.

L	X	L	J	V	M	L	S	W
K	G	H	G	R	A	S	U	A
L	F	C	N	C	L	U	O	C
L	T	F	I	Y	K	O	I	K
N	C	M	S	D	V	R	R	Y
Q	O	R	U	K	M	O	A	K
C	T	Z	M	Q	M	M	L	L
Q	R	P	A	V	K	U	I	D
Z	A	N	Y	R	Z	H	H	R

A ______________________________

C ______________________________

H ______________________________

H ______________________________

W ______________________________

Z ______________________________

Name ______________________________

Me ready to hunt thesaurus!

Thesaurus Hunt

Use a thesaurus to find a synonym for each clue below.

So, when does the fun start?

Across

2. Run
3. Grab
7. Accident
8. Love
12. Melt
13. So
14. Jump
16. Skinny
17. Roomy
19. Cute
21. Calm
22. Food
24. Deceive
25. Dedicated
26. Shake

Down

1. Win
2. Fly
3. Eat
4. Storm
5. Beautiful
6. Amazing
8. Then
9. Delight (in)
10. Smart
11. Most
15. Leave
18. Mistake
19. Get
20. Swallow
23. Annoy

Name ______________________________

Presto! The Prefix

To help pronounce a word, we sometimes divide the word into **syl-la-bles**. To understand what a word means, we can divide the word into its **parts**.

Many words are made up of different parts. For instance. . .

- **Root:** the main part of a word
- **Prefix:** a part added to the beginning of a root word to change its meaning

Example: recount

The root word is **count.** The prefix **re-** means **"again."** So, **recount** means **"to count again."**

Match each prefix with a root word. Then match the new word with its meaning and write it on the chart. Follow the example.

Prefix	Root	Prefix + Root = Meaning	New Word
sub-	view	underwater	1. submarine
re-	scope	see before	2.
mini-	pact	the most	3.
micro-	marine	used to see very small objects	4.
maxi-	mum	see again	5.
anti-	view	substance that prevents freezing	6.
com-	freeze	packed tightly	7.
pre-	mum	least amount	8.

Use The Words!

Use some of the new words from the chart to complete these sentences.

❶ The ____________________ speed on that road is 30 miles per hour.

❷ Dr. Frankenstone looked into her ____________________ to see the tiny cell.

❸ I think I'll ____________________ my notes so I can ace the test!

❹ We got to ____________________ the movie before everyone else.

❺ Putting ____________________ in your radiator will help save your car in winter.

Name ______________________________

Negative Prefixes

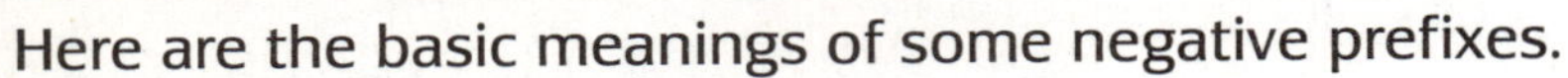

Is it really so unbelievable that I'm so undecided?

A **negative prefix** changes a word's meaning to the opposite of what it was.

Here are the basic meanings of some negative prefixes.

un- : not; opposite of
in- : not
de- : remove; do the opposite of
dis- : do the opposite of; not
non- : not; without

An Un-Positive Chart

Choose a negative prefix from the list above. Add it to each word to make a new word. Write the new word next to its matching definition.

PREFIX	WORD TO CHANGE	NEW WORD'S MEANING	NEW NEGATIVE WORD
	decided	not decided	1. undecided
	acceptable	not acceptable	2.
	believable	not believable	3.
	visible	not visible	4.
	complete	not complete	5.
	sensitive	not sensitive	6.
	active	not active	7.
	activated	not activated	8.
	caffeinated	not caffeinated	9.
	advantage	not an advantage	10.
	able	not able	11.
	agree	not agree	12.
	alcoholic	not alcoholic	13.
	perishable	not perishable	14.
	smoker	not a smoker	15.

Name ______________________________

Positively Negative

Fill in the blanks with words from the box. Note: All words begin with negative prefixes.

THE BOX

deactivate **inactive** **nonsmoker**

decaffeinated **insensitive** **invisible**

disagreed **nonperishable** **undecided**

unbelievable **incomplete** **unacceptable**

1. A box of Uncle Cheesey's Noodle Magic lasts forever. It is a ____________________ food item.
2. My brother said I was ____________________ because I made the dog sit in the rain.
3. We had a huge argument. Everyone ____________________ with me.
4. " ____________________ the engines before we hit the force field!" shouted Captain Picknot.
5. I'm the only one who can see my ____________________ friend.
6. Mom seems less grumpy when she drinks ____________________ coffee.
7. My dad doesn't cough so much since he became a ____________________.
8. Your story is ____________________. All you wrote was the title!
9. "If you remain ____________________, you will become a major blob!" Dr. Dobey stated.
10. Standing on your head and barking like a dog is ____________________ behavior at school.

Just because I use negative prefixes a lot doesn't mean I'm a negative person!

BONUS: Write two sentences using the leftover words.

1. ____.

2. ____.

Name ______________________________

Extraordinary Prefixes

Some **prefixes** are super-fun to use! They add special meaning to ordinary words!

Match Up! **Use a dictionary to match each Extraordinary Prefix with its meaning. Write the correct letter on the blank before each prefix.**

Extraordinary Prefixes	Meanings
_______ **1.** uni-	**a.** more than usual or way too much; sometimes used as a word that means "overactive"
_______ **2.** mega-	**b.** distant; far off
_______ **3.** techno-	**c.** a tremendous amount of; even more than enough
_______ **4.** inter-	**d.** between or among
_______ **5.** ultra-	**e.** extremely small; a billionth part
_______ **6.** trans-	**f.** very large; sometimes used on its own
_______ **7.** omni-	**g.** one or single
_______ **8.** auto-	**h.** all
_______ **9.** tele-	**i.** across; beyond
_______ **10.** extra-	**j.** half or partly
_______ **11.** bio-	**k.** back, behind, or backward; sometimes used as a word that means "from the past"
_______ **12.** semi-	**l.** use of skill and machines; sometimes used as a word to describe a type of modern dance music
_______ **13.** nano-	**m.** self
_______ **14.** retro-	**n.** outside; beyond
_______ **15.** hyper-	**o.** life

I'm getting ***ultra-hyper*** just thinking about ***mega-cool*** prefixes!

Name ______________________________

Be a Suffix Sleuth

If you're looking for trouble, you came to the right place!

Some suffixes can be pretty sneaky.
To break their code, concentration is key.

Now let's track down some of the most wanted suffixes.

Use the Sneaky Suffix Definitions to help you solve the crossword.

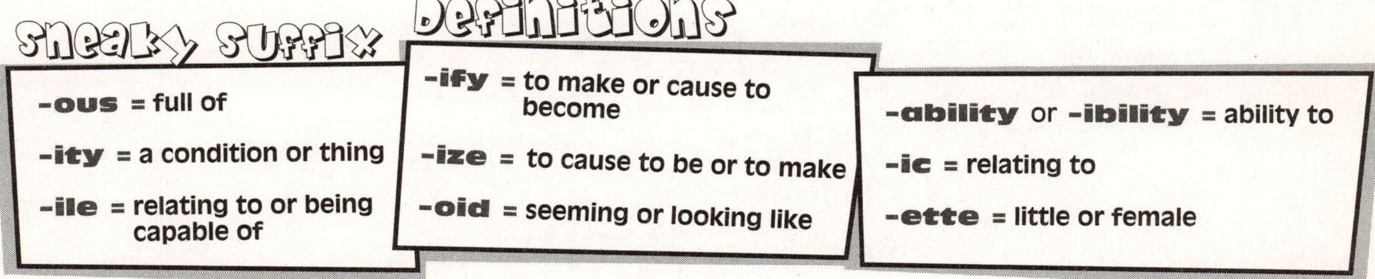

Sneaky Suffix Definitions

-ous = full of

-ity = a condition or thing

-ile = relating to or being capable of

-ify = to make or cause to become

-ize = to cause to be or to make

-oid = seeming or looking like

-ability or **-ibility** = ability to

-ic = relating to

-ette = little or female

Across

1. To make capital (as in a letter)
4. To make beautiful
11. Relating to an allergy
13. Condition of what is real
14. To make more special or specific
16. To make by means of a computer
17. Ability to be flexible
19. Condition of being elastic
21. Condition of being mobile
23. Relating to poetry
25. Seeming like an ape

Down

2. Electric power
3. Female usher
5. Full of adventure
6. Thing that can be projected
7. Full of glory
8. Relating to an infant
9. Cause to form crystals
10. To make intense
12. Small kitchen
15. State of being active
18. Full of thunder
20. Relating to history; having importance in history
22. Seeming like an oval
24. State of being odd

Name ______________________________

Let's Get Retro!
Suffix Review

Hey there!

Let's play it again!

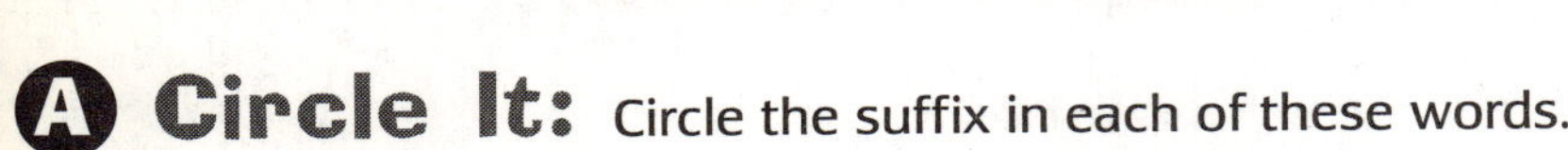

A Circle It: Circle the suffix in each of these words.

fearless **electricity** **anthropoid** **psychology** **neighborhood**

guitarist **allergic** **crystallize** **invasion** **African**

B Vocabu-Math: Combine each root with its suffix to create a new word.

1. history + ic = ______________________
2. mobile + ity = ______________________
3. India + an = ______________________
4. intense + ify = ______________________
5. adventure + ous = ______________________

C Re-shuffle: Unscramble the word parts to create new words. Write the words in the Correct-O column. Then circle each suffix.

Shuffle Word Parts			Correct-O
ib	ility	flex	1.
iend	fr	ly	2.
ng	dom	ki	3.
hood	chi	ld	4.
thun	ous	der	5.
get	ful	for	6.

D Fill in the Blanks: Use the words from the Correct-O column to complete these sentences.

1. The audience gave Rock Bohunk a ______________ ovation.
2. Sorry I missed your birthday. I'm a bit ______________ .
3. I thought that three-headed monster was ______________, but he chased me around the block.
4. That acrobat has incredible ______________.
5. "My ______________ should be called a queendom," announced Queen Gasserella.
6. Grandpa nodded and said, "Yep, in my ______________ I used to eat nails for breakfast."

E Supersonic Crossword

Across

6. Process of multiplying
7. The quality of being good
8. One who dances
9. Belonging to or relating to Italy

Down

1. Condition of being a member
2. State of being friends
3. One who talks
4. One who runs
5. The quality of being kind

F Suspicious Suffixes: Match each root word with a suffix. Then match the word to its meaning. Write the code for your answer in the Code Repository. We did the first one for you.

Root Word	Suffix	Meaning
1. usher	A. -ile	I. Office worker who meets visitors and answers the phone
2. computer	B. -ful	II. To make functional with a computer
3. reception	C. -ize	III. An association of boys or men
4. brother	D. -less	IV. Like a baby
5. great	E. -ist	V. The action of breaking
6. real	F. -age	VI. A female who escorts people to their seats at a show
7. break	G. -ness	VII. Showing no fear
8. fear	H. -hood	VIII. State of being real or factual
9. infant	I. -ity	IX. Quiet; peaceful
10. rest	J. -ette	X. Abundance; power

Code Repository

1. J. VI	3.	7.
2.	4.	8.
	5.	9.
	6.	10.

Name: ______________________________

Suffixes

A Multiple Choice:

Score: ____ /50

Circle the best meaning for each suffix.

1. -ette	**a.** little	**b.** female	**c.** large	**d.** a and b
2. -oid	**a.** cause to be	**b.** seeming like	**c.** full of	**d.** without
3. -ify	**a.** related to	**b.** cause to become	**c.** one who does	**d.** area of study
4. -ist	**a.** process or action	**b.** condition or special rank	**c.** one who practices or does	**d.** belonging to
5. -logy	**a.** area of study	**b.** full of	**c.** without	**d.** condition
6. -an or -ian	**a.** female	**b.** a collection	**c.** belonging to (from)	**d.** all of these
7. -ous	**a.** ability to	**b.** cause to become	**c.** one who does	**d.** full of
8. -age	**a.** collection, group	**b.** small	**c.** seeming like	**d.** process or action
9. -less	**a.** imitation	**b.** full of	**c.** without	**d.** small
10. -tion or -sion	**a.** special rank	**b.** process or action	**c.** area of study	**d.** without

B Apply the Suffix:

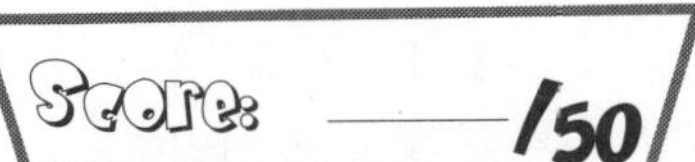

Add a suffix to the italicized word to fill in the blank correctly.

1. When you show *courage*, you are ____________________.
2. If you are good at *poetry*, you are ____________________.
3. If you can *concentrate* for a long time, you have good ____________________.
4. If you are from *Mexico*, you are ____________________.
5. Something shaped like an *oval* can be described as ____________________.
6. When you lack *fear*, you are ____________________.
7. A person who studies *biology* is called a ____________________.
8. When you ____________________ something, you give it *beauty*.
9. Things that are *elastic* have ____________________.
10. When you make things more *intense*, you ____________________ them.

Name ______________________________

Eponyms: It's All in the Name!

An **eponym** is a word that came from a person's name.

Eponym Word Chart

1. **Graham cracker:** Sylvester Graham baked up the first batch of these tasty crackers in the early 1800s. He called them a "health food."
2. **Caesar salad:** Caesar Cardini threw together this snappy salad in Tijuana, Mexico, back in 1924.
3. **Diesel:** Although it still needed a lot of tinkering, the first diesel engine was invented in the late 1800s by Rudolph Diesel.
4. **Derby:** In 1780 Edward Stanley, the 12th Earl of Derby, sponsored a race. Soon his name was used to mean "a premier horse race." Think Kentucky Derby.
5. **Frisbee:** In the 1920s Joseph Frisbie made pies near Yale University. Often, students would buy his pies and keep the plates to throw to each other. Soon the Frisbee as we know it today was invented.
6. **Guillotine:** Dr. Joseph-Ignace Guillotin (1738–1814) did not invent the guillotine. He was just trying to suggest a more humane way to behead prisoners.
7. **Jacuzzi:** Candido Jacuzzi created a system of underwater jets in a bathtub to give his ailing son *hydrotherapy* (water massage) at home.
8. **Leotard:** This form-fitting one-piece elastic garment got its name from French trapeze artist Jules Léotard in the mid-1800s.
9. **Levi's:** In 1872, tailor and businessman Levi Strauss made overalls and pants for miners out of canvas because the material was so strong and durable.
10. **Maverick:** Samuel Maverick was a Texas cattle owner who did not like to brand his cattle or keep them cooped up. This was different from what others were doing but he didn't care what others thought of him.
11. **Melba toast:** Late 19th-century opera singer Dame Nellie Melba got very sick. Part of her get-well diet included very dry, crisp, thinly sliced toast.
12. **Mesmerize:** Franz Anton Mesmer, a German doctor, tried to cure sick people through their unconscious mind. He called his hypnosis technique *mesmerism*.

(continued)

13. **Pasteurize:** Louis Pasteur, a French chemist in the 19th century, discovered a process of using heat to destroy harmful germs in perishable foods without hurting the food (such as milk).

14. **Sandwich:** As the story goes, sandwiches became popular when John Montagu, 4th Earl of Sandwich, took a bite of one. This 18th-century royal chap supposedly ate sandwiches while working and playing.

15. **Sideburns:** This face fuzz was originally named after Civil War General Ambrose Everett Burnside.

16. **Tupperware:** Developed by Earl Tupper in 1945, these popular plastic containers keep food fresh.

Hint: You'll find all the answers in the Eponym Word Chart.

Across

1. Beheading device
4. Premier horse race
9. Brand of jeans
10. Cardini's vegetable mix
13. A system of underwater jets in a bathtub
14. Rudolph invented this engine in the late 1800s
15. Earl's container helps keep food fresh
16. A TV show might do this to you

Down

2. Jules wore this as he flew through the air with the greatest of ease
3. Originally considered a healthy food choice
5. The Royal Earl ate it "on the run"
6. The opera singer's cure
7. You may be this, if you "go your own way"
8. Louis did this to kill germs
11. Facial hair named after a Civil War general
12. A flying pie plate

Name ______________________________

WOW! Palindromes!

A **palindrome** is a word that reads the same forward or backward.

Unscramble these palindromes.

bbi	1.	**add**	5.	**edde**	9.
ott	2.	**wwo**	6.	**omm**	10.
epep	3.	**otot**	7.	**obb**	11.
udd	4.	**oonn**	8.	**vee**	12.

Pick a Palindrome: Come up with three of your own palindromes.

______________________ ______________________ ______________________

Search for 18 palindromes below. As you find them in the Word Search, check them off at the bottom of the page.

C	L	R	R	T	W	K	Y	G	R	L	T	S
S	A	G	A	S	W	R	A	D	M	E	D	T
C	R	S	Z	R	N	L	E	Y	N	T	R	A
X	L	E	O	V	Y	I	N	E	A	E	L	T
R	T	M	V	L	F	V	T	G	F	K	T	S
V	A	F	M	I	O	P	L	E	M	L	L	R
R	T	D	E	M	V	S	R	A	L	L	N	E
O	C	D	A	K	X	E	D	M	L	E	J	D
T	I	H	B	R	R	A	R	T	D	V	L	D
A	V	C	L	O	M	W	Q	L	F	E	P	E
T	I	M	T	D	E	W	E	D	R	L	T	R
O	C	O	R	A	C	E	C	A	R	W	Q	G
R	R	R	N	R	E	P	A	P	E	R	P	F

civic: to do with community	**redder:** more red	**repaper:** to paper again
racecar: car for racing	**sagas:** many adventure stories	**stats:** numbers representing data
rotator: something that spins	**kayak:** Inuit canoe	**madam:** formal term for a lady
deified: idolized or adored	**refer:** to pass on information	**reviver:** one who refreshes
radar: detection device	**solos:** more than one solo	**tenet:** a rule or theory
rotor: spinning device	**level:** flat or balanced	**dewed:** sprinkled lightly with water

Name ______________________________

What an Oxymoron!

An **oxymoron** is a combination of contradictory words.

Get this: Check out these oxymoron examples.

Evaporated milk If the milk is evaporated, how can it still be there?

Front end What's that? The front or the end?

Each sentence has half an oxymoron. Find the other half of the oxymoron in the Oxymoron Ice Oven. Use each word once.

1. Fred was a **paid** __________________ at our charity dance.
2. Your **loud** __________________ was heard across the room.
3. How can you be wearing **baggy** __________________?
4. **"Never** __________________!" Matilda yelled as she bungeed off the bridge.
5. At 199 pounds, Sugar Pop Wheeler is a **light** __________________.
6. I'd say you had **even** __________________ of winning.
7. Wrap up that bread tightly or it will get **freezer** __________________.
8. Is that **jumbo** __________________ too big for you to eat?
9. Everyone knows about that. That's **old** __________________.
10. That magician is a **real** __________________.

tights	news
odds	again
heavyweight	volunteer
burn	shrimp
phony	whisper

Name ________________________________

Let's Get Retro!
Eponym and Palindrome Review

An **eponym** is a word that ________________________________.

A **palindrome** is a word that ________________________________.

ID, Please!

Identify each of the following as an eponym (E) or a palindrome (P).

_____ 1. rotor

_____ 2. tenet

_____ 3. frisbee

_____ 4. deified

_____ 5. diesel

_____ 6. levis

_____ 7. kayak

_____ 8. jacuzzi

_____ 9. leotard

_____ 10. solos

Do It Your Way!

Write five palindromes.

1. ______________________
2. ______________________
3. ______________________
4. ______________________
5. ______________________

Who's What? **Beside each person's name, identify the eponym he or she helped create.**

1. Edward Stanley ______________________
2. Dame Nellie Melba ______________________
3. Louis Pasteur ______________________
4. John Montagu ______________________
5. Gen. A.E. Burnside ______________________
6. Earl Tupper ______________________
7. Franz Mesmer ______________________
8. Joseph-Ignace Guillotin ______________________
9. Sylvester Graham ______________________
10. Caesar Cardini ______________________

Name: ____________________

Quickie Quiz

Eponyms, Palindromes, Oxymoron

A Definitions: Write a definition for each term.

Score: ____ /30

1. **Eponym:** ____________________.
2. **Palindrome:** ____________________.
3. **Oxymoron:** ____________________.

B Multiple Choice

Score: ____ /20

Is the entry an eponym, palindrome, or oxymoron? Check the appropriate column.

ENTRY	EPONYM	PALINDROME	OXYMORON
1. kayak			
2. frisbee			
3. graham cracker			
4. neat mess			
5. jumbo shrimp			
6. freezer burn			
7. repaper			
8. diesel			
9. sandwich			
10. mesmerize			

C Write a Palindrome

Score: ____ /20

Write five palindromes that do not appear on this test.

1. ____________________
2. ____________________
3. ____________________
4. ____________________
5. ____________________

D Eponym or Oxymoron

Score: ____ /30

Write the most suitable EPONYM or OXYMORON in the blank.

1. She is a ____________________ because she does what she thinks is best.
2. We ____________________ milk so it lasts longer.
3. The acrobat is wearing a purple ____________________.
4. When the principal entered the room, there was a deafening ____________________.
5. I'm starting to get a numb ____________________ in my leg.
6. Ugh! This ice cream has freezer ____________________.

Name ____________________

Sound Out Homophones

Homophones are words that sound the same, but have different spellings and meanings.

You won't get bored when you're on board.
Be off to the Homophone Zone and become a Homophone Master!

Fill in the blank with the correct homophone.

Level 1: The Start-O-Sphere

1. (*bare*, *bear*) That ________ is ________. He has no hair!
2. (*ate*, *eight*) I ________ ________ donuts.
3. (*paws*, *pause*) Perhaps I should ________ to look at my dog's ________.
4. (*past*, *passed*) In the ________, stories were ________ by word of mouth.
5. (*tail*, *tale*) Grandpa told us a ________ about the monkey with the longest ________.
6. (*threw*, *through*) Johnny ________ the ball ________ the window.
7. (*there*, *they're*) I said, "________ in ________!"
8. (*worn*, *warn*) I should ________ you that your tires are ________ out.

Level 2: The Not-Bad-O-Sphere

1. (*write*, *right*) I'll ________ with my ________ hand. You can use your left.
2. (*so*, *sew*) Dad asked, "________, do you want to learn how to ________?"
3. (*inn*, *in*) Come ________ to the ________ and stay a while.
4. (*Sunday*, *sundae*) It's ________; let's have an ice cream ________!
5. (*steal*, *steel*) Stop! Don't ________ the ________!
6. (*karat*, *carrot*) We'd be rich if that ________ was twenty-four ________ gold!
7. (*break*, *brake*) Use the bike's ________ or you will ________ something.
8. (*serial*, *cereal*) I watch a TV ________ while I eat my ________.

Level 3: The Sweet-O-Sphere

1. (*are*, *our*, *hour*) ________________ time has come. The magic ________________ is here.
2. (*missed*, *mist*) I could not see you in the ________________, so I ________________ you.
3. (*your*, *you're*) Mom said, "________________ not going out until ________________ work is done."
4. (*whether*, *weather*) ________________ the ________________ is good or not, we're going.
5. (*hole*, *whole*) How do you know if that's a ________________ ________________ or just part of one?
6. (*rowed*, *rode*, *road*) Winky ________________ on the ________________ while Dinky ________________ the boat.
7. (*scent*, *cent*, *sent*) I spent every ________________ you ________________ as soon as I smelled that ________________.
8. (*bye*, *by*, *buy*) I'll come ________________ later to ________________ some cake. ________________, see you then!

Level 4: The Wow-O-Sphere

1. (*do*, *dew*, *due*) __________ you know that the morning __________ is __________ right about now?
2. (*too*, *to*, *two*) You __________ can come __________ see me in my tutu, __________.
3. (*knot*, *naught*, *not*) That is ________________ the way to tie a ________________ in this contest, so your score is ________________.
4. (*there*, *their*, *they're*) Look at __________ house over __________. That's where __________ staying.
5. (*pear*, *pair*, *pare*) Please ________________ the ________________. Do that twice and you will have a ________________.
6. (*towed*, *toad*; *toe*, *tow*) Wow, that giant ________________ ________________ the ________________ truck with its ________________!
7. (*herd*, *heard*; *hear*, *here*) I ________________ the ________________ of elephants and now I ________________ you ________________, too.
8. (*knows*, *nose*; *blew*, *blue*; *gnu*, *new*, *knew*) I ________________ that a ________________ ________________ ________________ his ________________ ________________ when he ________________ he should. (more than one correct answer)

Name ______________________________

Home in on Homographs

Homographs are words that are spelled the same but have different meanings and pronunciations.

Each clue contains two definitions. Read each clue and decide what homograph fits both meanings.

Clues

Across

1. To bend forward from the waist; front of a ship; weapon that shoots arrows
5. A numeral or quantity; more numb
7. Prisoner; to find guilty
10. To pardon or forgive someone; an "explaining why" reason
11. Hot, sandy region that gets little rain; to abandon
12. White bird (symbol of peace); jumped off (usually into water)
14. To rip; a drop of clear liquid emitted by the eye
16. To shut; near

Down

2. To injure; coiled up
3. Without a mistake; to make without a mistake
4. To coil up; moving air
6. Sixty seconds; very, very tiny
7. The way you behave; to direct as with a symphony orchestra
8. An agreement (that is usually signed); to shrink, opposite of expand
9. To show the way; a metallic element
13. A thing; to disagree (as in court)
15. To start again; a record of work experience and education

Name ______________________________

Commonly Confused Words

Read the definitions. Place the correct commonly confused word in each blank.

among: used with more than two items
between: used with two items

1. I will dance ______________ the many tulips in my garden.
2. If you're playing goalie, stand ______________ the posts of the net.

fewer: used when counting individual parts; smaller number; often used before a plural noun
less: smaller amount; not as much; often used before a singular noun

3. Gronk has ______________ hair than Blerk.
4. Blerk has ______________ rocks than Gronk.

affect: a verb that means to change or influence
effect: a noun that means the result of an action

5. If you are kind, it will ______________ everyone around you.
6. That song has such an ______________ on me every time I hear it.

assure: guarantee **ensure:** make certain
insure: guard against loss or damage

7. You can't drive your car until you ______________ it.
8. I ______________ you that the doors are locked.
9. Please ______________ that your lips remain closed.

formally: correctly, ceremoniously
formerly: before

10. Soula ______________ signed the contract in front of her lawyer.
11. ______________ a famous musician, he now sells insurance.

precede: come before
proceed: go to

12. Please ______________ to the visitation center immediately.
13. The queen will ______________ the king in this procession.

good: an adjective that describes a noun as being positive
well: an adverb that means to do an action positively

14. You are doing very ______________!
15. Morty is a ______________ boy.

metal: a chemical element such as copper or iron
medal: award

16. That ring is made from a precious ______________.
17. You deserve a ______________ for all your hard work.

access: a way to get to
excess: too much, more than enough

18. Yikes! The ______________ milk spilled all over the place.
19. You'll find ______________ to the laboratory through that trap door.

assistance: help
assistants: helpers

20. Dr. Gub, I will need your ______________ to complete the operation.
21. All of the ______________ are having a meeting.

Name ______________________________

Put It in Context

Many times you can figure out what a word means by the way it is used in a sentence. This skill is called *Using Context Clues*.

- Loquacious Mrs. Lipflapper spoke for three hours nonstop.

Loquacious? Is that a flower in your mother's garden? Guess again. From the sentence and the way **loquacious** is used, we can guess that it might mean **tends to talk a lot**.

Using Context Clues

Read each sentence below. Select the meaning that best suits the sentence.

❶ The **gargantuan** dragon towered above brave knight Sir Run-a-lot.

a. mean **b.** scary **c.** huge **d.** fire-breathing **e.** hairy

❷ My mother uses the **maxim**, "If at first you don't succeed, try, try again." So I won't give up.

a. sentence **b.** saying **c.** word **d.** question **e.** poem

❸ In **antiquity**, people had to hunt and gather for all of their food.

a. caves **b.** ancient times **c.** antique cars **d.** arctic weather **e.** war time

❹ **Magnanimous** Uncle Shlitzy always gave his money to people who needed help.

a. happy **b.** peaceful **c.** patient **d.** dumb **e.** generous

❺ Sorry to be so **incredulous**, but you haven't proven anything to me yet.

a. sleepy **b.** angry **c.** disbelieving **d.** unfriendly **e.** alert

Choose three words from above. Using the words, write three new sentences to demonstrate their meanings.

1. ______________________________
2. ______________________________
3. ______________________________

Name: ______________________________

QUICKIE QUIZ

Homophones, Homographs, and More

A ~~Knotty~~ Naughty Homophone Zone:

Circle the 10 incorrect homophones. Write the correct words below.

All write! Tell me now. Which which is which? I no you no. I'm knot moving until you tell me. I can stand hear for an our. It's not fare four you two trick me like this!

1. ______________________________
2. ______________________________
3. ______________________________
4. ______________________________
5. ______________________________
6. ______________________________
7. ______________________________
8. ______________________________
9. ______________________________
10. ______________________________

B Conquer the Homographs!

The words in *italics* are pronunciations of homographs. Sound out each word and spell it correctly in the Homograph Detention Center.

1. Have your *REH-zoo-may* with you when you apply for that job.
2. I will practice until I *purr-FECT* that skill.
3. That vault is made of solid *LED*.
4. Look carefully for all *MI-noot* details.
5. We must never *dih-SIRT* people who need help.
6. She's standing at the ship's *BAU*.
7. I can't feel anything; my hand is *NUM-mer*.
8. I *WOWND* the yarn into a ball.
9. Hank just *DOHV* into a pool.
10. Please *ik-SKYUZ* my brother.

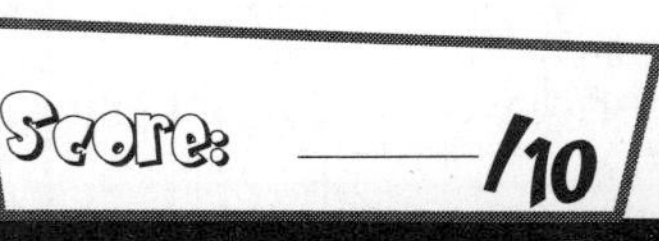

Homographs Detention Center	
1.	6.
2.	7.
3.	8.
4.	9.
5.	10.

C Commonly Confused Words:

Score: ____ /35

Fill in the blanks with the correct words.

1. (*medal*, *metal*) That ____________ case will protect your ____________.
2. (*assure*, *ensure*, *insure*) I ____________ you, it is safe!
3. (*affect*, *effect*) Did that medicine ____________ you like it did me?
4. (*less*, *fewer*) There are ____________ oceans than there are lakes.
5. (*good*, *well*) Hooray, your performance went ____________!
6. (*assistants*, *assistance*) My ____________ will hold you down.
7. (*access*, *excess*) The ____________ is spilling out.

D Use Context Clues:

Score: ____ /35

Read the sentences below. Choose the best meaning for each underlined word

❶ Since the accident, he never laughs anymore. He seems so **lugubrious**.

a. stubborn **b.** courageous **c.** weird **d.** gloomy **e.** cheerful

❷ He was so **obsequious**, he would dust off the seat before his boss sat down.

a. serious **b.** friendly **c.** happy **d.** smart **e.** too eager to please

❸ You're **insatiable**! When will you stop eating?

a. stubborn **b.** friendly **c.** funny **d.** serious **e.** always wanting more

❹ It is very **quotidian** for people to eat lunch around noon.

a. common **b.** special **c.** unusual **d.** surprising **e.** different

❺ I know you're trying to **usurp** all my pieces when I'm not looking.

a. hide **b.** seize **c.** paint **d.** break **e.** repair

❻ He's so **incredulous**, it doesn't matter how much proof you show him.

a. disbelieving **b.** angry **c.** sleepy **d.** serious **e.** alert

❼ That **connoisseur** knows everything there is to know about art.

a. idiot **b.** expert **c.** artist **d.** student **e.** part-timer

Cool!

Name ______________________________

The Synonym/Antonym Analogy Adventure

Word analogies express the relationship between words. They connect ideas.

Rain is to summer as snow is to winter

A **synonym** is a word that has the same or nearly the same meaning as another word.

skinny = thin **jump = hop** **purchase = buy**

So this is what a ***Synonym Analogy*** could look like:

Admirable is to **fantastic** as **awful** is to **horrible**

An **antonym** has the opposite or nearly the opposite meaning as another word.

fast ≠ slow **up ≠ down** **give ≠ take**

So this is what an ***Antonym Analogy*** could look like:

Funny is to **sad** as **sweet** is to **sour**

Wow, I think I get this!

Choose words from the Word Vault to complete each analogy. Circle synonym or antonym to indicate the type of analogy. Use a dictionary!

1. *Big* is to *huge* as *tiny* is to ______________ **synonym antonym**
2. *Brave* is to *meek* as *fearful* is to ______________ **synonym antonym**
3. *Nice* is to *pleasant* as *fast* is to ______________ **synonym antonym**
4. *Happy* is to *joyful* as *skillful* is to ______________ **synonym antonym**
5. *Finished* is to *incomplete* as *intact* is to ______________ **synonym antonym**
6. *Pretty* is to *attractive* as *strong* is to ______________ **synonym antonym**
7. *Fall* is to *tumble* as *jump* is to ______________ **synonym antonym**
8. *Negative* is to *affirmative* as *ordinary* is to ______________ **synonym antonym**

Word Vault

adept	remarkable	minuscule	daring
broken	speedy	hurdle	powerful

Name ________________________________

The Relationship Analogy Adventure

I thought I was connected.

Music is to notes as poetry is to words

comparison...correlation...correspondence... equivalence...likeness...parallel...relation...resemblance

Check this out!

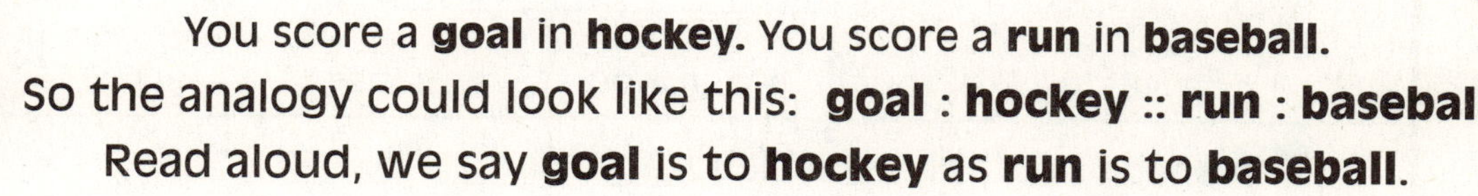
You score a **goal** in **hockey.** You score a **run** in **baseball.**
So the analogy could look like this: **goal** : **hockey** :: **run** : **baseball**
Read aloud, we say **goal** is to **hockey** as **run** is to **baseball.**

Beethoven was a **classical** composer about 200 years ago.
Eminem is a **rapper** now.
So the analogy could look like this: **Beethoven** : **classical** :: **Eminem** : **rap**

Try this!

Choose the best answer and write it in the blank.

1. banana : peel :: nut : ____________________

   a. coat **b.** shell **c.** hat **d.** wings

2. oil : fry :: water : ____________________

   a. boil **b.** roast **c.** swim **d.** fish

3. car : vehicle :: stove : ____________________

   a. kitchen **b.** cook **c.** hot **d.** appliance

4. Italian : language :: Italy : ____________________

   a. food **b.** continent **c.** country **d.** place

5. dance : waltz :: ice cream : ____________________

   a. frozen **b.** cone **c.** flavor **d.** vanilla

6. baby : human :: cub : ____________________

   a. animal **b.** bear **c.** furry **d.** trainer

(continued)

7 fish : salmon :: dog : ________________

a. poodle **b.** bark **c.** furry **d.** cat

8 second : minute :: inch : ________________

a. foot **b.** worm **c.** mile **d.** meter

9 captain : team :: chief : ________________

a. boss **b.** tribe **c.** leader **d.** president

10 soft : feel :: sweet : ________________

a. taste **b.** touch **c.** tongue **d**. sense

11 spoon : utensil :: golf club : ________________

a. golf ball **b.** sports equipment **c.** swing **d.** driver

12 jungle : tiger :: arctic : ________________

a. polar bear **b.** cold **c.** tropical **d.** lion

13 swim : water :: run : ________________

a. summer **b.** jump **c.** ice **d.** land

14 book : nonfiction :: movie : ________________

a. fiction **b.** true **c.** cartoon **d.** documentary

15 mom : dad :: aunt : ________________

a. uncle **b.** friend **c.** sister **d.** woman

Now you're getting into the groove!

16 bear : fur :: human : ________________

a. hair **b.** shorts **c.** woman **d.** bald

17 snow : white :: sky : ________________

a. rain **b.** blue **c.** cloud **d.** weather

18 drum : percussion :: flute : ________________

a. air **b.** instrument **c.** woodwind **d.** music

19 plumber : wrench :: photographer : ________________

a. picture **b.** photograph **c.** camera **d.** film

20 food : solid :: water : ________________

a. drink **b.** beverage **c.** solid **d.** liquid

Name ______________________________

I. still feel the connection!

The "Part of" Analogy Adventure

As we have learned, word analogies express relationships between words. Analogies associate, bridge, cohere, conjoin, link, marry (you get the picture!) ideas.

In the **"Part of" Analogy Adventure**, you will go through these **Thinking Steps:**

Step 1: READ the analogy.

Step 2: THINK of the **RELATIONSHIP**; for example, between **lung** and **human**.

Step 3: THINK: A human uses a lung to breathe.

Step 4: CHECK the list of selections and **CHOOSE** the analogy that seems to have the same relationship. **HINT:** Eliminate the answers you are sure are wrong.

Try it! Lung is to human as ______________ **is to** ______________

Lung : human ::

a. tail : horse **b.** nose : ear **c.** brother : gas **d.** gill : fish

If you picked "d," you are well on your way to success in the "Part of" Analogy Adventure!

The "Part of" Analogy Adventure Begins!

Choose the best answer and write it in the blanks.

1 house : closet :: ________________ : ________________

a. car : trunk **b.** light : switch **c.** camp : fire **d.** tree : wood

2 computer : printer :: ________________ : ________________

a. seed : melon **b.** remote : TV **c.** radio : speaker **d.** finger : hand

3 onion : skin :: ________________ : ________________

a. laces : shoes **b.** candy bar : caramel **c.** book : cover **d.** milk : cow

4 cat : fur ball :: ________________ : ________________

a. volcano : lava **b.** sneeze : cold **c.** laugh : joke **d.** rain : cloud

5. baseball : bat :: ____________ : ____________

a. needle : thread **b.** racquet : tennis **c.** comb : hair **d.** nail : hammer

6. flower : petal :: ____________ : ____________

a. melon : seed **b.** wire : lamp **c.** pizza : crust **d.** hand : finger

7. pizza : cheese :: ____________ : ____________

a. stamp : letter **b.** wall : paint **c.** flag : pole **d.** table : chair

8. seed : melon :: ____________ : ____________

a. tree : wood **b.** car : parking lot **c.** clothing : suitcase **d.** food : tray

9. pole : flag :: ____________ : ____________

a. needle : thread **b.** branch : leaf **c.** hammer : nail **d.** wall : paint

10. camera : film :: ____________ : ____________

a. oven : bread **b.** candles : cake **c.** cloud : rain **d.** engine : car

11. sand : beach :: ____________ : ____________

a. stars : sky **b.** gas : car **c.** jar : lid **d.** table : legs

12. dial : blender :: ____________ : ____________

a. melon : seed **b.** lamp : light bulb **c.** plug : toaster **d.** switch : light

13. plastic : doll :: ____________ : ____________

a. wood : table **b.** keys : car **c.** oar : boat **d.** tree : root

14. vapor : gas :: ____________ : ____________

a. gas : car **b.** water : liquid **c.** tap : water **d.** picture : frame

15. door : garage :: ____________ : ____________

a. toothbrush : teeth **b.** wire : lamp **c.** mouth : face **d.** light bulb : room

Name: ______________________

QUICKIE QUIZ **Analogies**

Score: ____/100

Wow, check out this one-time offer!

Get the greatest analogy hits ever...

Remember that big #1 hit "Synonym/Antonym Analogies" ?
How about that chart scorcher "'Part of' Analogies"?
And who could ever forget "Relationship Analogies" ?
You get these fresh funkables and much more in the...

Extreme Analogy Groovathon!

1 end : beginning :: ________________ : ________________

a. heart : brain **b.** lose : win **c.** high : higher **d.** front : side

2 melt : thaw :: ________________ : ________________

a. fast : faster **b.** walk : trot **c.** sad : unhappy **d.** right : left

3 mechanic : wrench :: ________________ : ________________

a. needle : doctor **b.** hose : saddle **c.** barber : scissors **d.** cat : dog

4 hammer : nail :: ________________ : ________________

a. saw : wood **b.** bit : drill **c.** screwdriver : screw **d.** shovel : dirt

5 song : singer :: ________________ : ________________

a. piano : player **b.** painting : painter **c.** skip : rope **d.** runner : run

6 lake : water :: ________________ : ________________

a. house : brick **b.** bread : butter **c.** swimmer : lake **d.** fish : swim

7 water : wet :: ________________ : ________________

a. flame : hot **b.** tap : water **c.** dark : light **d.** dog : bark

8 hole : drill :: ________ : ________

a. throw : ball **b.** skate : slide **c.** cut : saw **d.** tape : measure

9 fruit : pie :: ________ : ________

a. pages : book **b.** cookie : sweet **c.** hot : cold **d.** flower : spring

10 astronomer : stars :: ________ : ________

a. chef : cook **b.** doctor : nurse **c.** driver : car **d.** detective : clues

11 butler : maid :: ________ : ________

a. bat : ball **b.** rooster : hen **c.** chef : cook **d.** doctor : dentist

12 cub : bear :: ________ : ________

a. egg : bird **b.** chick : chicken **c.** cat : lion **d.** horse : pony

13 Sunday : Monday :: ________ : ________

a. beginning : end **b.** winter : summer **c.** afternoon : evening **d.** build : house

14 army : soldier :: ________ : ________

a. game : player **b.** student : classroom **c.** music : dancer **d.** club : member

15 sugar : candy :: ________ : ________

a. sugar : coffee **b.** fruit : juice **c.** flour : bread **d.** music : dance

16 fungus : mushroom :: ________ : ________

a. tree : bark **b.** team : Yankees **c.** animal : baby **d.** insect : cricket

17 hive : bee :: ________ : ________

a. web : spider **b.** hay : horse **c.** dog : house **d.** rock : cave

18 allowed : aloud :: ________ : ________

a. permission : noise **b.** right : write **c.** thunder : storm **d.** take : give

19 bat : swing :: ________ : ________

a. punch : bow **b.** run : jump **c.** ball : throw **d.** kick : goal

20 time : rhyme :: ________ : ________

a. watch : catch **b.** hype : byte **c.** done : bone **d.** fun : son

Answer Key

Ha! Ha! FUNNY Word Search (p. 7)

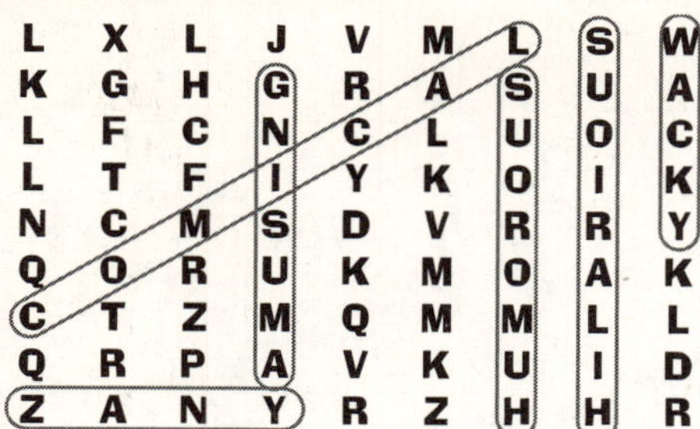

amusing comical hilarious humorous wacky zany

Thesaurus Hunt (p. 8)

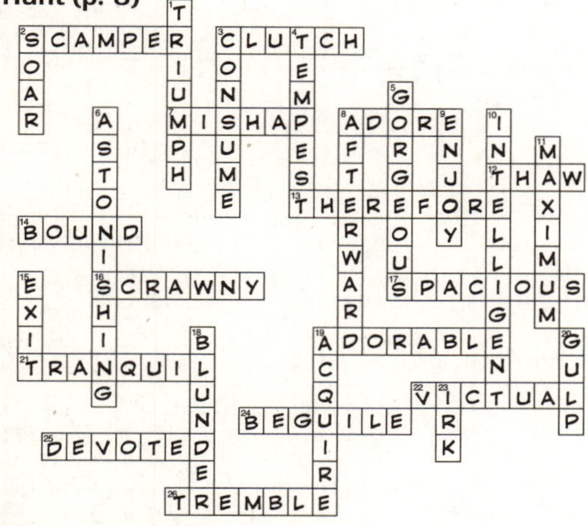

Presto! The Prefix (p. 9)

Match Up!

1. submarine
2. preview
3. maximum
4. microscope
5. review
6. antifreeze
7. compact
8. minimum

Use the Words!

1. maximum
2. microscope
3. review
4. preview
5. antifreeze

Negative Prefixes (p. 10)

2. unacceptable
3. unbelievable
4. invisible
5. incomplete
6. insensitive
7. inactive
8. deactivated
9. decaffeinated
10. disadvantage
11 disable
12. disagree
13. nonalcoholic
14. nonperishable
15. nonsmoker

Positively Negative (p. 11)

1. nonperishable
2. insensitive
3. disagreed
4. Deactivate
5. invisible
6. decaffeinated
7. nonsmoker
8. incomplete
9. inactive
10. unacceptable

BONUS: Answers will vary, but should use *unbelievable* and *undecided*.

Extraordinary Prefixes (p. 12)

1. g
2. f
3. l
4. d
5. c
6. i
7. h
8. m
9. b
10. n
11. o
12. j
13. e
14. k
15. a

Ultra-Cool X-Word (p. 13)

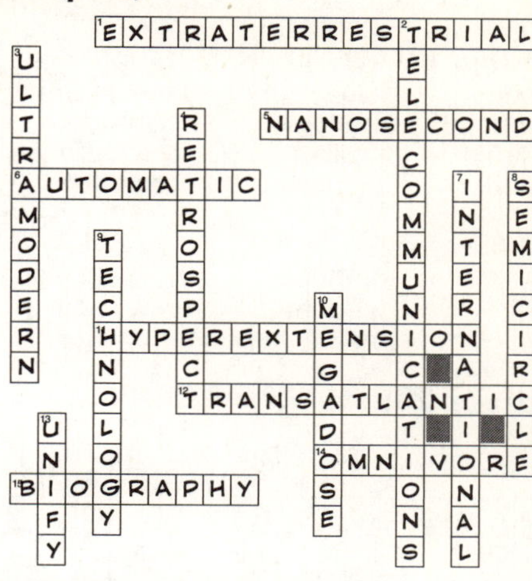

Let's Get Retro! Prefix Review (pp. 14–15)

A. What's Your "Prefix-ability"?

1. c
2. d
3. c
4. b
5. c
6. c
7. b
8. a
9. a
10. b

B. Pre-fix It!

1. omni-
2. un-
3. nano-
4. in-
5. auto-
6. retro-
7. Com-
8. re-
9. inter-
10. tele-

C. What's It Mean?

1. intergalactic
2. autograph
3. omnivorous
4. nanosecond
5. retrospect
6. compressing
7. inactive
8. telecommunications
9. redecorate
10. unbelievable

D. Find It!

1. hyper
2. extra
3. micro
4. ultra
5. semi
6. mega
7. auto
8. de

Box of Meanings

semi – half or partly
hyper – more than usual or way too much
auto – self
ultra – a tremendous amount, possibly more than enough
mega – very large
extra – outside; beyond
de – remove
micro – incredibly small

Quickie Quiz: Prefixes (p. 16)

A. Multiple Choice

1. d
2. d
3. c
4. d
5. a
6. c
7. b
8. b
9. c
10. b

B. Match

1. c
2. d
3. a
4. j
5. g
6. i
7. b
8. e
9. f
10. h

C. Identify

1. hyper-
2. pre-
3. ultra-
4. uni-
5. retro-
6. dis-
7. in-
8. tele-
9. mini-
10. de-

Suffix Rocks! (p. 17)

1. greatness
2. fearless
3. friendly
4. dancer
5. kindness
6. forgetful
7. talker, runner

Suffix Math (pp. 18–19)

sisterhood, neighborhood, membership, citizenship
biology, sociology, Brazilian, American
multiplication, institution, percussionist, specialist
orphanage, postage

Smart Suffixes

1. -ship
2. -ist
3. -logy
4. -hood
5. -dom
6. -ist
7. -an, -ian
8. -tion
9. -age
10. -hood

X-Word-ology (p. 20)

Quickie Unscramble: vegetarian, geology

Be a Suffix Sleuth (p. 21)

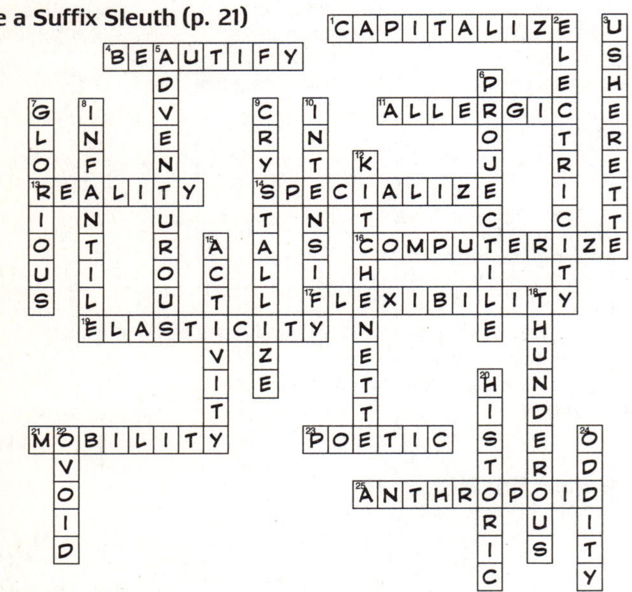

Let's Get Retro! Suffix Review (pp. 22–23)

A. Circle It

-less, -ity, -oid, -logy, -hood, -ist, -ic, -ize, -sion, -an

B. Vocabu-Math

1. historic
2. mobility
3. Indian
4. intensify
5. adventurous

C. Re-Shuffle

1. flexibility
2. friendly
3. kingdom
4. childhood
5. thunderous
6. forgetful

D. Fill in the Blanks

1. thunderous
2. forgetful
3. friendly
4. flexibility
5. kingdom
6. childhood

E. Supersonic Crossword

F. Suspicious Suffixes

1. J. VI.
2. C. II.
3. E. I.
4. H. III.
5. G. X.
6. I. VIII.
7. F. V.
8. D. VII.
9. A. IV.
10. B. IX.

Quickie Quiz: Suffixes (p. 24)

A. Multiple Choice

1. d
2. b
3. b
4. c
5. a
6. c
7. d
8. a
9. c
10. b

B. Apply the Suffix

1. courageous
2. poetic
3. concentration
4. Mexican
5. ovoid
6. fearless
7. biologist
8. beautify
9. elasticity
10. intensify

Eponym X-Word (p. 26)

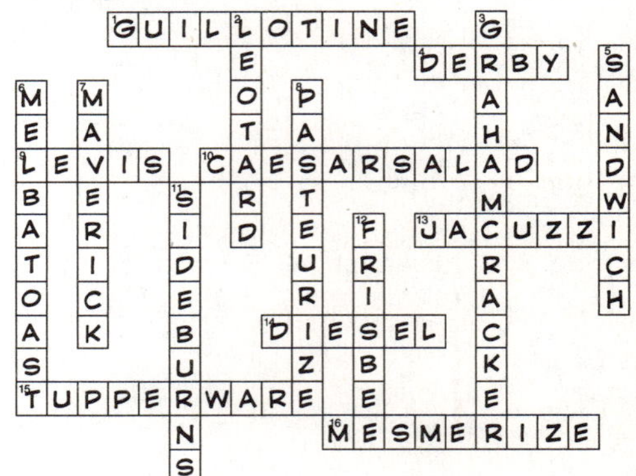

WOW! Palindromes! (p. 27)

Pop the Palindromes

1. bib
2. tot
3. peep
4. dud
5. dad
6. wow
7. toot
8. noon
9. deed
10. mom
11. bob
12. eve

Palindrome Finder

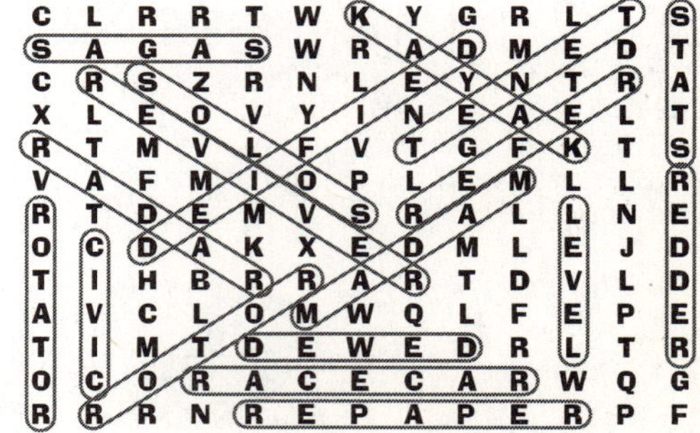

What an Oxymoron! (p. 28)

1. volunteer
2. whisper
3. tights
4. again
5. heavyweight
6. odds
7. burn
8. shrimp
9. news
10. phony

Let's Get Retro! Eponym and Palindrome Review (p. 29)

An eponym is a word that came from a person's name. A palindrome is a word that reads the same forward or backward.

ID, Please!

1. P
2. P
3. E
4. P
5. E
6. E
7. P
8. E
9. E
10. P

Who's What?

1. derby
2. melba toast
3. pasteurize
4. sandwich
5. sideburns
6. Tupperware
7. mesmerize
8. guillotine
9. graham cracker
10. Caesar salad

Quickie Quiz: Eponyms, Palindromes, Oxymoron (p. 30)

A. Definitions

1. Eponym: a word that came from a person's name
2. Palindrome: a word that reads the same forward or backward
3. Oxymoron: an expression with contradictory words

B. Multiple Choice

1. palindrome
2. eponym
3. eponym
4. oxymoron
5. oxymoron
6. oxymoron
7. palindrome
8. eponym
9. eponym
10. eponym

C. Write a Palindrome

Answers will vary.

D. Eponym or Oxymoron

1. maverick
2. pasteurize
3. leotard
4. silence
5. feeling
6. burn

Sound Out Homophones (pp. 31–32)

Level 1

1. bear, bare
2. ate, eight
3. pause, paws
4. past, passed
5. tale, tail
6. threw, through
7. They're, there
8. warn, worn

Level 2

1. write, right
2. So, sew
3. in, inn
4. Sunday, sundae
5. steal, steel
6. carrot, karat
7. brake, break
8. serial, cereal

Level 3

1. Our, hour
2. mist, missed
3. You're, your
4. Whether, weather
5. whole, hole
6. rode, road, rowed
7. cent, sent, scent
8. by, buy, Bye

Level 4

1. Do, dew, due
2. two, to, too
3. not, knot, naught
4. their, there, they're
5. pare, pear, pair
6. toad, towed, tow, toe
7. heard, herd, hear, here
8. Answers may vary, but could be: knew, blue, gnu, blew, new, nose, knows

Home in on Homographs (p. 33)

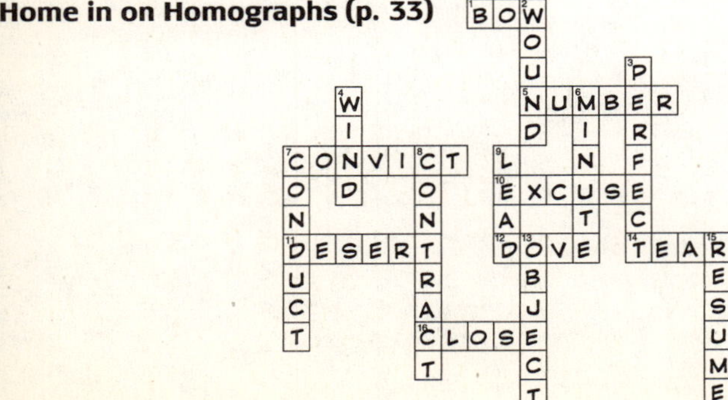

Commonly Confused Words (p. 34)

1. among
2. between
3. less
4. fewer
5. affect
6. effect
7. insure
8. assure
9. ensure
10. formally
11. Formerly
12. proceed
13. precede
14. well
15. good
16. metal
17. medal
18. excess
19. access
20. assistance
21. assistants

Put It in Context (p. 35)

1. c
2. b
3. b
4. e
5. c

Quickie Quiz: Homophones, Homographs, and More (pp. 36–37)

A. Naughty Homophone Zone

1. right
2. witch
3. know
4. know
5. not
6. here
7. hour
8. fair
9. for
10. to

B. Conquer the Homographs!

1. résumé
2. perfect
3. lead
4. minute
5. desert
6. bow
7. number
8. wound
9. dove
10. excuse

C. Commonly Confused Words

1. metal, medal
2. assure
3. affect
4. fewer
5. well
6. assistants
7. excess

D. Use Context Clues

1. d
2. e
3. e
4. a
5. b
6. a
7. b

The Synonym/Antonym Analogy Adventure (p. 38)

1. minuscule / synonym
2. daring / antonym
3. speedy / synonym
4. adept / synonym
5. broken / antonym
6. powerful / synonym
7. hurdle / synonym
8. remarkable / antonym

The Relationship Analogy Adventure (pp. 39–40)

1. b
2. a
3. d
4. c
5. d
6. b
7. a
8. a
9. b
10. a
11. b
12. a
13. d
14. d
15. a
16. a
17. b
18. c
19. c
20. d

The "Part of" Analogy Adventure (pp. 41–42)

1. a
2. c
3. b
4. a
5. d
6. d
7. b
8. c
9. b
10. a
11. a
12. d
13. a
14. b
15. c

Quickie Quiz: Analogies (pp. 43–44)

1. b
2. c
3. c
4. c
5. b
6. a
7. a
8. c
9. a
10. d
11. b
12. b
13. c
14. d
15. c
16. d
17. a
18. b
19. c
20. d